Animal mothers

Bobbie Kalman

 Crabtree Publishing Company

www.crabtreebooks.com

Created by Bobbie Kalman

Author and Editor-in-Chief
Bobbie Kalman

Educational consultants
Elaine Hurst
Joan King
Jennifer King

Notes for adults
Jennifer King

Editors
Kathy Middleton
Crystal Sikkens

Design
Bobbie Kalman
Katherine Berti

Print and production coordinator
Katherine Berti

Prepress technician
Katherine Berti

Photo research
Bobbie Kalman

Photographs
BigStockPhoto: page 7
iStockphoto: page 12
Photos.com: page 10
Other photographs by Shutterstock

Library and Archives Canada Cataloguing in Publication

Kalman, Bobbie, 1947-
    Animal mothers / Bobbie Kalman.

(My world)
Issued also in electronic format.
ISBN 978-0-7787-9555-1 (bound).--ISBN 978-0-7787-9580-3 (pbk.)

    1. Parental behavior in animals--Juvenile literature. 2. Animals--Infancy--Juvenile literature. I. Title. II. Series: My world (St. Catharines, Ont.)

QL762.K343 2011   j591.56'3   C2010-907432-7

Library of Congress Cataloging-in-Publication Data

Kalman, Bobbie.
  Animal mothers / Bobbie Kalman.
      p. cm. -- (My world)
    ISBN 978-0-7787-9580-3 (pbk. : alk. paper) -- ISBN 978-0-7787-9555-1 (reinforced library binding : alk. paper) -- ISBN 978-1-4271-9662-0 (electronic (pdf))
    1. Parental behavior in animals--Juvenile literature. 2. Animals--Infancy--Juvenile literature. I. Title.
    QL762.K35 2011
    591.56'3--dc22
                                              2010047637

Crabtree Publishing Company

www.crabtreebooks.com   1-800-387-7650

Printed in China/022011/RG20101116

Published in Canada
Crabtree Publishing
616 Welland Ave.
St. Catharines, Ontario
L2M 5V6

Published in the United States
Crabtree Publishing
PMB 59051
350 Fifth Avenue, 59th Floor
New York, New York 10118

Published in the United Kingdom
Crabtree Publishing
Maritime House
Basin Road North, Hove
BN41 1WR

Published in Australia
Crabtree Publishing
386 Mt. Alexander Rd.
Ascot Vale (Melbourne)
VIC 3032

Words to know

calf

chick

cub   duckling

fawn   foal

galloping   joey

kit   kitten   pouch

Some animal mothers
take care of their babies.
This mother duck is taking care
of her **ducklings**.

Some animal mothers
bring food to their babies.
This mother bird
is bringing a fish to her **chick**.

Some animal mothers feed
their babies milk from their bodies.
Cat mothers feed their **kittens** milk.

Fox mothers also feed their **kits** milk from their bodies.

Some animal mothers help their babies stand up and walk. This mother deer is helping her **fawn** take its first steps.

Some animal mothers teach
their babies how to run.
This pony mother is **galloping**,
or running fast, with her **foal**.

Some animal mothers move their babies often to keep them safe. This cougar mother carries her **cub** by the back of its neck.

Some animal mothers
carry their babies
in **pouches**.
Kangaroo mothers
carry their **joeys**
in pouches.
Joeys are
baby kangaroos.

pouch

Some animal
mothers hug
their babies.
This wallaby
mother is hugging
her joey.

Some animal mothers
kiss their babies.
This dog mother is kissing her puppy.

What are these animal mothers
doing with their babies?

The elephant mother
is washing her **calf**.

The cat mother
is cleaning her kitten.

The lynx mother
is playing with her cub.

The polar bear mother
and her cub
are taking a nap.

Notes for adults

Objectives
- to teach children how animal mothers take care of their young
- to teach the names of baby animals
- to acquaint children with the different activities that animal mothers and their young share
- to have children explore the different ways their mothers take care of them and the activities they do together

Before reading the book
Ask these questions:
"What do baby animals need?"
"What do you need?"

As you read each page of the book
Ask the children:
"What is this animal mother doing?" (feeding, nursing, cleaning, watching, teaching, protecting, carrying, hugging, kissing, playing, etc.)
"What do you think baby animals do?" (listen, eat, follow, learn, care, love)
"Why do baby animals need their mothers?"
"Why do you need your mother?"

Activities
Prepare a set of cards for each child with animal and baby animal names.

Ask the children to match each animal name with its baby's name. Make it challenging by putting the cards face down and asking the children to match the animals from memory.

Have the children mimic the sounds of the baby animals. Multicultural connection: If you have children from different countries, ask them to make the animal sounds the way they hear them and say them in their languages.

Extension
Bobbie Kalman's *It's fun to learn about baby animals series* will help children expand their knowledge of the lives of baby animals. Children will learn about animals' bodies, classifications, life cycles, homes, how their mothers care for them, and some funny things they do.
The series has a book on each of the following baby animals: chipmunks, lemurs, polar bears, wolves, bunnies, elephants, foxes, giraffes, pigs, raccoons, wild and pet puppies, horses, cats, apes, deer, and bears. There are also books about baby reptiles, baby birds, caterpillars to butterflies, and tadpoles to frogs. All are at *Guided reading: J*. Learning about baby animals is fun because they are just plain adorable to look at!

For teacher's guide, go to www.crabtreebooks.com/teachersguides